THE
CHEROKEE
INDIANS

THE JUNIOR LIBRARY OF
AMERICAN INDIANS

THE
CHEROKEE
INDIANS

Nicole Claro

CHELSEA HOUSE PUBLISHERS
New York   Philadelphia

FRONTISPIECE: A Cherokee girl in ceremonial dress, photographed around 1900

CHAPTER TITLE ORNAMENT: A Cherokee mask depicting a buffalo man

Chelsea House Publishers
EDITOR-IN-CHIEF   Remmel Nunn
MANAGING EDITOR   Karyn Gullen Browne
COPY CHIEF   Juliann Barbato
PICTURE EDITOR   Adrian G. Allen
ART DIRECTOR   Maria Epes
DEPUTY COPY CHIEF   Mark Rifkin
ASSISTANT ART DIRECTOR   Noreen Romano
MANUFACTURING MANAGER   Gerald Levine
SYSTEMS MANAGER   Lindsey Ottman
PRODUCTION MANAGER   Joseph Romano
PRODUCTION COORDINATOR   Marie Claire Cebrián

The Junior Library of American Indians
SENIOR EDITOR   Liz Sonneborn

Staff for THE CHEROKEE INDIANS
COPY EDITOR   Laurie Kahn
EDITORIAL ASSISTANT   Michele Haddad
DESIGNER   Debora Smith
PICTURE RESEARCHER   Diana Gongora
COVER ILLUSTRATOR   Vilma Ortiz

9 8

Library of Congress Cataloging-in-Publication Data

Claro, Nicole.
   The Cherokee Indians/by Nicole Claro.
      p.   cm.—(The Junior library of American Indians)
   Includes index.
   Summary: Examines the history, culture, and future prospects of the Cherokee Indians.
   ISBN 0-7910-1652-8
   1. Cherokee Indians—Juvenile literature. [1. Cherokee Indians.
2. Indians of North America.] I. Title. II. Series.   90-23480
E99.C5C664 1991   CIP
973'.04975—dc20   AC

CONTENTS

CHAPTER 1

Beginnings   7

CHAPTER 2

The Principal People   13

CHAPTER 3

Changing Ways   23

CHAPTER 4

"Civilizing"   33
    the Cherokees

CHAPTER 5

The Trail of Tears   43

PICTURE ESSAY

Beautiful Objects   49

CHAPTER 6

Life in the West   59

CHAPTER 7

The Cherokees Today   67

Chronology   76

Glossary   77

Index   78

Statues of Kana'ti (left) and Selu, the first Cherokee man and woman

CHAPTER **1**

Beginnings

Long ago, all beings lived in the sky, which was made of solid rock. In time, the rock sky grew very crowded, so one day the water beetle went in search of a new world. He explored the vast sea under the sky but found no land. When he rose from the water to return home, he was covered with mud. The mud grew and grew until it formed a large island. This island became the Earth.

The buzzard flew from the sky to see if the muddy earth was dry enough to be a new home for animals. While investigating the island, he flapped his wings. Where his wings skimmed the damp earth, a valley was created. When he lifted them again, a mountain was formed.

When the earth was dry, the plants and animals came down and tried very hard to stay awake for seven days. Only a few, such as the owl and the panther, were able to do this. That is why these animals can see in the dark and hunt at night. Some plants, such as the pine, cedar, and holly, also stayed awake. That is why these plants stay green and beautiful all year-round.

The first man and woman were called *Kana'ti* and *Selu*. They had one son of their own. They also adopted a mysterious child whom they called Wild Boy. His parents tried to tame him but Wild Boy remained mischievous.

Kana'ti hunted for the family. He always came home with deer or turkey. The boys were curious about their father's occupation. One day they followed Kana'ti into the woods. They saw him approach a large rock and lift it up. Out from under the rock ran a fat buck, which Kana'ti shot with arrows he had made.

A few days later, the boys crept back to the rock. Like their father, they lifted it, but carelessly held it up too long. Instead of one deer, all the animals under the rock escaped. This is why hunters now must search all over the woods to find their prey.

Selu provided vegetables for the family. The boys followed her one day to find out where the vegetables came from. They saw her rub her stomach and armpits. Suddenly, a basket she had placed in front of her was filled with corn and beans. The boys were terrified. Believing that their mother was a witch, they decided that they had no choice but to kill her.

Selu learned of their plans. Instead of being angry, she bravely gave her sons special instructions to follow after her death. She told them to drag her body along a patch of cleared ground seven times. If they did this, the field would be covered with cornstalks in the morning. But the boys were lazy and dragged their mother's body over the land twice. That is why corn needs to be tended and grows only in certain spots.

These stories have been told for centuries by the *Ani-Yun'wiya*, the Principal People. The Ani-Yun'wiya are now known as the Cherokee Indians. For most of their history, the Cherokees lived in a lush, beautiful territory in what is now the southeastern United States. This land was their home for at least a thousand years before white people began to journey to North America.

· TRADITIONAL CHEROKEE TERRITORY ·

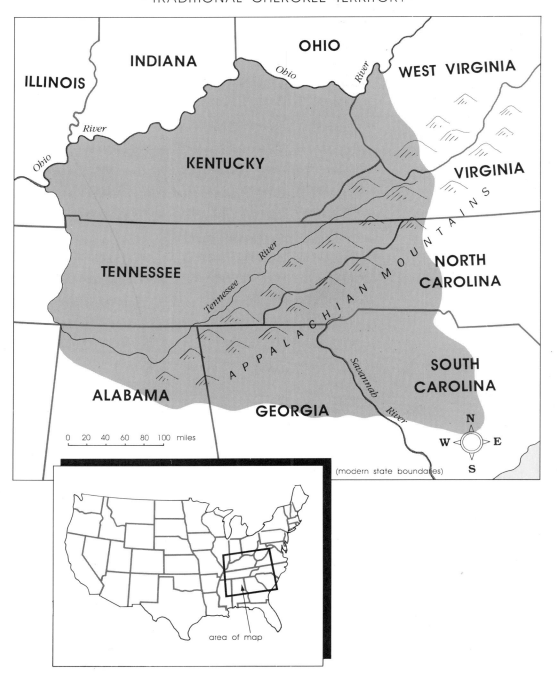

Some Cherokees still live in the homeland of their ancestors. Some make their home hundreds of miles away in Oklahoma. And some live in cities throughout the United States. But Cherokees everywhere continue to enjoy learning about Kana'ti, Selu, and the beginning of the world. To the Cherokees, these stories are not just entertaining tales. They are also the early history of their people. Hearing the ancient stories of the past makes them proud to be Cherokees today. ▲

Three women, photographed in the early 1900s, wearing traditional Cherokee clothing

CHAPTER **2**

The Principal People

The Cherokees' stories are just one way to learn about their ancient history. Another way is to examine the tools and other objects made by Cherokees long ago. By studying these items, scientists called anthropologists have been able to piece together a picture of how the Cherokees lived in the past.

Long ago, the Cherokee people built large villages. Many stretched for miles along the banks of a river. In the center of each village was a council house made of saplings and mud. Here, people gathered for parties, political assemblies, and religious ceremonies.

13

Clustered around the council house was a collection of homesteads. Usually grandparents, parents, and children lived together. To house all of these relatives, homesteads had to have several buildings. These included a large, rectangular summer house; a small, round winter house (an *asi*); and several storage cribs.

In every Cherokee village, there lived people of different *clans*. A clan was a large group of relatives who believed they descended from one common ancestor. Clan membership was very important. It helped shape people's sense of who they were. It also affected their relationships with others. For instance, a person's clan determined whom she or he could and could not marry. Men and women of the same clan were not allowed to wed because they were thought to be very closely related.

Cherokee children always belonged to their mother's clan. Because of this, a woman's brothers played a larger role in rearing her offspring than her husband did. Although Cherokee fathers loved their children, they were members of different clans and therefore were not thought to be related by blood.

Girls and boys came to understand how to behave by watching their elders. A disobedient child was never spanked. Instead, the youngster might be lightly scratched with thorns as a punishment. Sometimes a mother would merely shame a misbehaving child with gentle teasing.

By observing adults, children also learned about the work they would do when they grew up. In Cherokee society, women and men had different duties to perform. However, the work of both sexes was considered equally important.

Women were responsible for tending their family's crops of corn, beans, and pumpkins. Often, they carried their youngest children to the fields with them. Infants were strapped into a kind of portable crib called a cradleboard. Placed under the shade of a tree, children in cradleboards could happily watch their mothers, aunts, and grandmothers perform their farming chores.

When the corn was ripe, the *Green Corn Ceremony* was held. During the ceremony, women prepared a great feast. They pounded the corn and separated the chunks from the meal. The chunks were added to stews and soups. The cornmeal was baked into bread. Sometimes, women mixed chestnuts or dried beans into the dough to make their bread especially tasty.

Women also made many objects used by the Cherokees every day. From saplings, they built benches for their homes. From river cane and honeysuckle, they wove baskets. And from clay, they molded pots, which they then placed on open fires to dry and harden.

Sewing was another responsibility of Cherokee women. Using needles made of bone, they assembled skirts, cloaks, and moccasins from tanned deerskins. Women did not need to spend a great deal of time sewing, however. Most of the year, the climate was so warm that adults wore little and children usually wore nothing at all. Even in the winter, the Cherokees did not need many clothes. They spent much of the time in their warm asis, where they always kept a fire burning.

Among the duties of Cherokee men was hunting for food. During the winter, they would travel far from home in search of deer, turkey, and bears. When they found their prey, they killed the animals using bows, arrows, traps, and blowguns.

Cherokee men were also fishermen. They first trapped fish by building a dam in a stream. Next, they stunned the animals by stirring a natural poison, such as ground horse chestnuts, into the water. The men could then simply scoop up the paralyzed fish. When they opened the dam, the other fish would recover and swim away.

Playing games helped keep men fit and strong for their long winter hunts. The most popular was stick ball, which was similar to

Long ago, the Cherokees lived in small round houses (left) in the winter and in large rectangular houses in the summer.

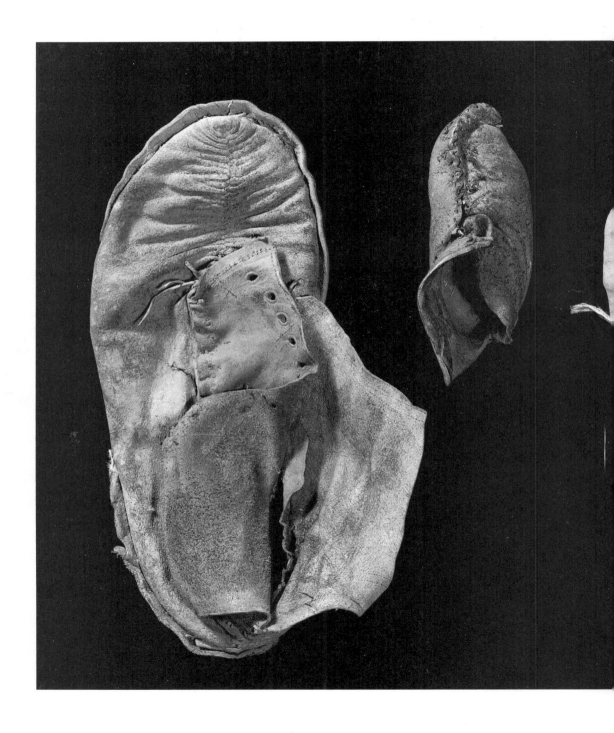

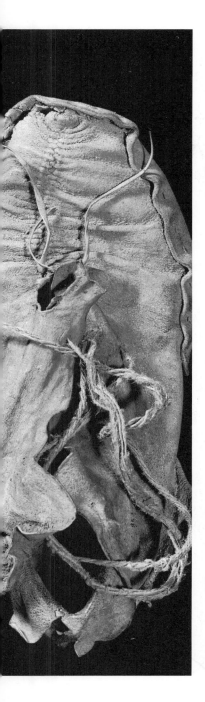

the modern sport of lacrosse. Players used a wooden racket to throw a hard deerskin ball across the other team's goal line. The game was so competitive that Cherokees called stick ball "the little brother to war."

Waging war was another activity of Cherokee men. The decision to go to war, however, was made by both men and women during meetings in the council house. The only reason they would choose to fight was to seek revenge if a Cherokee had been killed by someone from another tribe. The Cherokees believed that after death a person's spirit went to a place called the Darkening Land. If the person had been murdered, it was thought that his or her spirit could not rest there until the murderers were also killed.

War parties were made up of anywhere between 2 and 100 men. For several days, they prepared for war in the council house by fasting and sipping a special tea called black drink. Walking in single file, they then

The Cherokees traditionally wore moccasins that women sewed out of deerskin.

traveled to the enemy's territory. Each warrior stepped inside the footprints of the man in front of him to make their path difficult to track. The Cherokees always tried to take their enemies by surprise.

Some Cherokee women joined in war parties. These War Women cooked food and carried firewood and water for the warriors. They were also in charge of any captives taken by the men. Sometimes the War Women adopted captured women and children. Most captives, however, were burned at the stake. Torturing captives was thought to help send dead spirits to the Darkening Land.

Killing people who had murdered others made the Cherokees feel that they were keeping the world in balance. They tried to maintain this balance in other ways as well. For instance, when a hunter killed a deer, the tribe performed a ritual. During the ritual, the hunter apologized to the spirit of the deer. He explained that he had hunted only to feed his family. The Cherokees felt it was wrong to kill any more animals than was absolutely necessary.

The Green Corn Ceremony also was performed to restore order to the world. As a part of this annual ritual, people cleaned their homesteads and the council house.

They also forgave any wrongs committed by others during the previous year. By the end of the Green Corn Ceremony, every Cherokee could look ahead to the future with a clean slate.

The Cherokees' way of life made sense to them. Their environment provided them with food, shelter, and clothing. Their kin and religious ceremonies gave them comfort and a sense of well-being.

The Europeans who began to travel to the Cherokee homeland in 1540 saw the Indians' society differently. They disapproved of the Cherokee way of life because it was so unlike their own. For instance, the Europeans thought Cherokee men were lazy and Cherokee women were treated like slaves. They did not see that men needed to play games in order to be good hunters and that women had great power in Cherokee society. Instead of trying to understand Cherokee customs, many of the foreigners decided they were worthless. These people then set out to destroy the way of life the Principal People loved. ▲

The Spanish explorer Hernando de Soto traveled through Cherokee territory in 1540.

CHAPTER 3

Changing Ways

For almost 1,000 years, the Principal People lived alone on their land. In this time, Cherokee culture evolved gradually. But when Europeans arrived in their homeland, everything began to change fast and furiously.

In 1540, Hernando de Soto, a Spanish explorer, became the first European to pass through Cherokee territory. Accompanied by a huge party of soldiers, slaves, and animals, de Soto had come in search of gold mines. He grew furious when all he found were Cherokee farming villages. Before leaving the region, de Soto ordered his men to torture and slaughter many of the Indians. Because the Cherokees were not Chris-

23

tians, the Spaniards did not believe they were entitled to humane treatment.

The killing spree was a disaster for the Cherokees. But even worse was the effect of diseases that the Europeans had brought with them. The Cherokees had never before been exposed to smallpox, bubonic plague, and measles. As a result, they had no natural resistance to them. The Cherokees turned to their traditional healers for help. However, the plants and words that the healers usually used to cure the ailing did little to relieve these new illnesses. Large numbers of Cherokees died in epidemics.

In the 1700s, the Cherokees met a different group of Europeans—the English. Unlike the Spanish, the English had come in peace. They were traders and offered European-made goods, such as metal farming tools, that the Indians had never seen before. In exchange, the Cherokees gave the English deerskins, which they then sold to other Europeans for profit.

The Cherokees were pleased with their new tools. They were easier to use and more durable than the tools the Indians used to make from stone. In order to get more of these goods, Cherokee hunters killed larger numbers of deer than ever before. Hunting more animals than they themselves needed, the Indians were abandoning their old idea of the importance of keeping the world balanced.

The English traders also changed the Cherokees' ideas about war. In the past, the Indians had gone into battle only for revenge. Now, the Cherokees began to wage war in order to take war captives. They could trade the captives to the English, who sold them to landowners as slaves.

The Cherokees were drawn into wars between the English and their European enemies as well. Spanish and French people were settling in other parts of North America. Each of these groups of Europeans wanted to control the entire continent. They were continually fighting, each group hoping to drive the other two out. All three powers allied themselves with Indian tribes, who provided warriors to help the Europeans fight their battles. The most intense fighting occurred between 1754 and 1763. These battles are now called the French and Indian War because most Indians sided with France.

The Choctaw and the Iroquois Indians were allied with the French. Because the Cherokees were friendly with the English, the Cherokees feared these two large Indian groups would attack them. The English

A portrait of Cherokee chief Cunne Shote, painted by English artist Francis Parsons in 1762

promised to protect the Cherokees from the French-allied Indians. In exchange, the Cherokees promised to support the English in their battles in the Ohio River valley.

Cherokee warriors traveled northward toward the battle sites, but had to turn back because of bad weather. On their way home, they came upon some grazing cows. The hungry warriors assumed the animals were wild. They killed the cows and ate the meat.

The cows actually had belonged to English farmers. When the farmers discovered what the Cherokee men had done, they attacked the warriors and scalped several of them. The tribe retaliated by attacking English settlements.

In November 1759, representatives of the English met with 32 Cherokee chiefs at Fort Prince George in South Carolina. The chiefs' mission was to restore the Cherokee-English alliance. Although the Indians came in peace, the angry English imprisoned 29 of them. When Cherokee chief Oconostota attacked the fort in February, the English soldiers immediately murdered their unarmed prisoners.

For the next two years, the Cherokees and the English fought each other in a series of bloody battles. During this time, one-half of the Cherokees died. Some were killed in the fighting. Many more died of hunger and disease. In addition, countless Cherokee villages were destroyed.

The English won the French and Indian War. They gained control of the vast territory in North America that had been claimed by

Austenaco, a Cherokee chief, led a force of 100 warriors in the French and Indian War.

the French. The English also forced the Cherokees to give up a large amount of their hunting territory. This loss of land only added to the disasters that the fighting had brought to the Cherokee people.

Another war—the American Revolution—broke out in 1775. The conflict was between the English settlers in North America and the English government. But once again the Cherokees were drawn into the fighting. They sided with the English government because the English settlers—who now called themselves Americans—were trying to take even more of the Indians' territory.

In the summer of 1776, the Cherokees attacked American settlements in Georgia, Virginia, and the Carolinas. The Americans then invaded the Cherokees' villages, determined to demolish the Indians' communities. American troops led by General Griffith Rutherford killed and scalped many Cherokee women and men and sold their children into slavery. Many Indians fled into the mountains in terror. Those who stayed behind were left without food and shelter in the remains of 50 Cherokee villages.

The war ended in 1783 with an American victory. The Cherokees welcomed peace, but it came at a high price. The

An engraving of Charleston, South Carolina—one of the largest cities founded in the Southeast by European settlers and traders

Americans made the tribe surrender a huge amount of its land to the newly formed United States.

In nearly 250 years of contact with whites, the Cherokees had faced constant turmoil. War and disease had devastated their way of life. But now they looked ahead to a peaceful future. They had lost many of their people and much of their territory. They were confident, though, that their peace with the Americans would gain them some security at last. ⏶

Cherokee Alphabet.

D_a	R_e	T_i	δ_o	O_u	i_v
$S_{ga}\ O_{ka}$	F_{ge}	Y_{gi}	A_{go}	J_{gu}	E_{gv}
δ_{ha}	P_{he}	$\mathcal{D}_{hi}$	F_{ho}	Γ_{hu}	$\mathcal{C}_{hv}$
W_{la}	$\mathcal{C}_{le}$	P_{li}	G_{lo}	M_{lu}	$\mathcal{A}_{lv}$
$\mathcal{F}_{ma}$	$\mathcal{U}_{me}$	H_{mi}	5_{mo}	y_{mu}	
$O_{na}\ t_{hna}\ G_{nah}$	Λ_{ne}	h_{ni}	Z_{no}	$\mathcal{A}_{nu}$	O_{nv}
T_{qua}	ω_{que}	P_{qui}	V_{quo}	ω_{quu}	$\mathcal{E}_{quv}$
$U_{sa}\ \omega_{s}$	4_{se}	b_{si}	$\ddagger_{so}$	$\mathcal{E}_{su}$	R_{sv}
$L_{da}\ W_{ta}$	$S_{de}\ \mathcal{C}_{te}$	$\mathcal{A}_{di}\mathcal{A}_{ti}$	Λ_{do}	S_{du}	$\mathcal{S}_{dv}$
$\mathcal{S}_{dla}\ \mathcal{C}_{tla}$	L_{tle}	C_{tli}	$\mathcal{I}_{tlo}$	$\mathcal{O}_{tlu}$	P_{tlv}
G_{tsa}	V_{tse}	h_{tsi}	K_{tso}	J_{tsu}	C_{tsv}
G_{wa}	ω_{we}	$\mathcal{O}_{wi}$	$\mathcal{O}_{wo}$	$\mathcal{I}_{wu}$	6_{wv}
ω_{ya}	β_{ye}	δ_{yi}	6_{yo}	G_{yu}	B_{yv}

The letters of the Cherokee alphabet created by Sequoyah

CHAPTER 4

"Civilizing" the Cherokees

The more contact the Cherokees had with whites, the more their traditional ways seemed to fade away. By the late 1700s, it appeared as though their culture was slowly disintegrating. Many Indians resisted these changes, but some Cherokees did not think that they were such a bad thing. These tribe members thought that the Cherokees should adopt some of the Americans' customs. They believed that the Americans would leave them alone only if the Cherokees behaved like them.

The U.S. government was eager to help the Cherokees adjust to the new ways. It wanted the Cherokees to give up hunting and live like American farmers. If the Indians did this, they would no longer have a use for their hunting territory. The United States hoped that it could then buy this excess land from the tribe. Government officials wanted to open the area to land-hungry American pioneers.

The U.S. government had another reason to be interested in the fate of the Cherokees. Some Americans truly wanted to help the Indians. These non-Indians believed that their way of life was the right way and thought that the Cherokees would be better off if they adopted white customs.

In the early 1800s, the United States began a policy of "civilizing" the Cherokees. U.S. officials believed a "civilized" person was a devout Christian who owned property, farmed land, and could read and write English. They sent men called agents to live among the Cherokees and teach them white ways.

From 1801 to 1823, the Cherokees' agent was Return J. Meigs. Meigs set up many programs intended to help the Cherokees. For the first time, things commonly found in American towns, such as fenced-in farms and blacksmith shops, began to appear in

The Cherokees presented this belt made of wampum (shell beads) to Agent Return J. Meigs.

Cherokee territory. Meigs gave plows to Cherokee men. Like American men, they, rather than their female relatives, were now supposed to do farm work. The agent gave spinning wheels and looms to Cherokee women. Like American women, they were expected to make clothing out of woven cloth instead of tanned deerskins. Just as the United States had hoped, Meigs also persuaded the Cherokees to sell some of their hunting territory.

At the same time, other whites, called missionaries, came to live with the Cherokees. The missionaries set up schools to teach the Indians how to read and write. But most of all, they wanted to convert the Indians to Christianity. Many Cherokee parents were willing to have their children schooled in English, but few wanted the students to forget their old religion.

Most missionaries established boarding schools. Their Indian students lived in dormitories rather than at home with their parents. The missionaries wanted to remove the children from the "bad" influence of their parents' culture.

In the new surroundings, they taught the youngsters many new things. In addition to academic subjects, such as English, arithmetic, and geography, the students were told to read the Bible, pray, and attend Christian religious services. Boys were instructed in plowing, planting, and other farming skills. Girls cooked, cleaned, and did other things the missionaries thought were proper for young ladies to do.

Many Cherokee children took very well to this new education. However, some of their behavior displeased their teachers. Swimming without clothing, playing loud, raucous games, and making crude jokes were common activities among young Cherokees. The missionaries knew that Cherokee parents rarely punished their children. They were afraid that if they spanked a student, the child's parents might remove him or her from school. So the teachers developed a new form of punishment: Disobedient children had to memorize Bible verses related to their misbehavior.

Reading and writing were new to Cherokee boarding-school students. Like most American Indians, the Cherokees had no way to write down words in their own language. During the *"civilization" movement*, however, a Cherokee man named Sequoyah became determined to create a Cherokee alphabet. He began his work in

1809. After 10 years of labor, he had developed 86 symbols that stood for Cherokee syllables. As a result, the Cherokees were one of the first Indian tribes to be able to read and write in their native language. In 1828, Elias Boudinot, a Cherokee who had been educated at mission schools, began publishing the *Cherokee Phoenix*, a newspaper in English and Cherokee.

The "civilization" movement also changed the way Cherokee adults made their living. Traditionally, the women in a family tended a small farm, growing just enough food to feed their household members. From agents and other whites, the Cherokees learned a new system of farming. Men took over the farm work and tried to harvest an excess of crops that could be sold to people outside their family. A successful farmer could make a large amount of money. In time, many Cherokees bought African slaves, built elegant houses, and expanded their small farms into plantations.

By 1808, many Cherokees had accumulated a great deal of property. That year, a council met to create a more formal legal system to protect this new wealth. The council created the first written Cherokee law. The law called for the formation of a

Robert Lindneux's 1940 portrait of the Cherokee leader Sequoyah

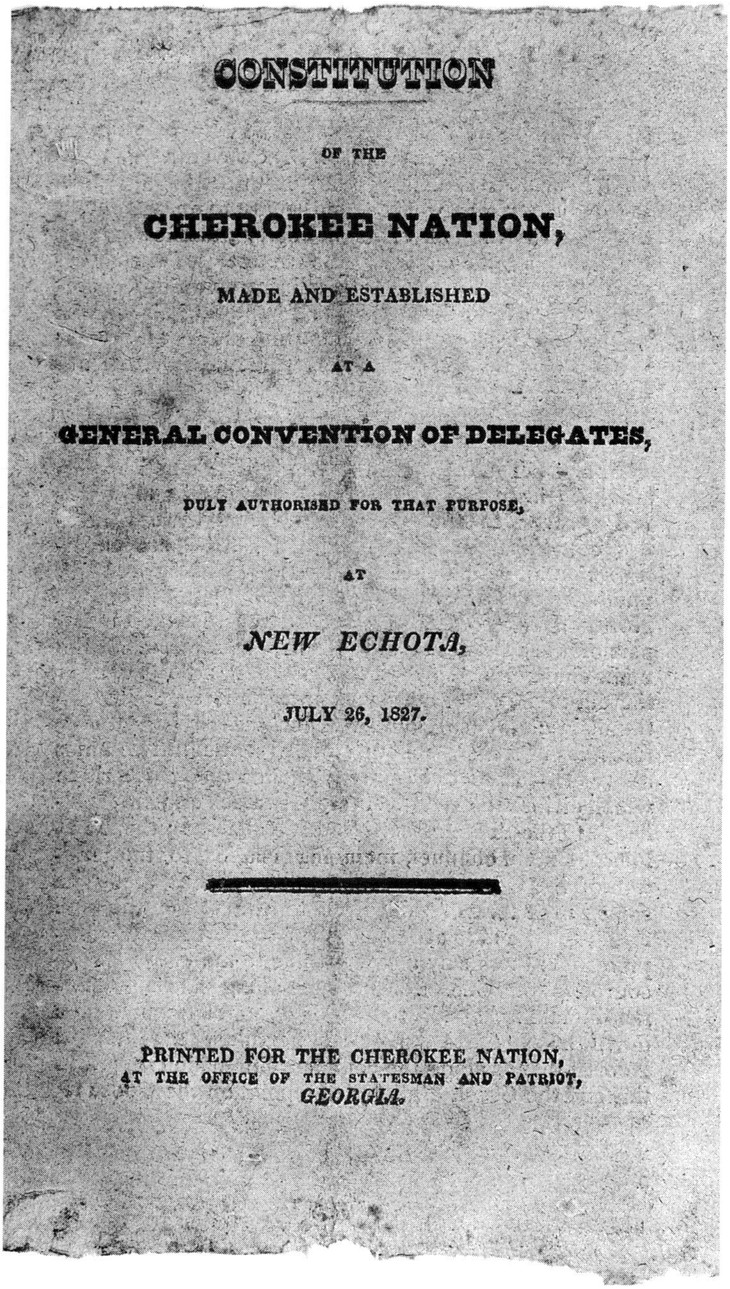

CONSTITUTION

OF THE

CHEROKEE NATION,

MADE AND ESTABLISHED

AT A

GENERAL CONVENTION OF DELEGATES,

DULY AUTHORISED FOR THAT PURPOSE,

AT

NEW ECHOTA,

JULY 26, 1827.

PRINTED FOR THE CHEROKEE NATION,
AT THE OFFICE OF THE STATESMAN AND PATRIOT,
GEORGIA.

The title page of the 1827 constitution of the Cherokee Nation

police force, known as the Lighthorse Guard.

Soon after, the Cherokees also reorganized their system of governing themselves. In 1827, they set down the rules of this new government in a constitution. This document was modeled after the United States Constitution. It stated that the Cherokees would be ruled by a General Council of elected representatives. Only Cherokee men would be permitted to vote.

The Cherokee constitution also defined the boundaries of their land. This provision made it clear that the Cherokees had no plan to expand their territory. More important, it showed that they intended to hold on to all of the land they still occupied.

The Americans had wanted the Cherokees to become "civilized." The Indians wrote a constitution like the whites. The Indians developed a written language like the whites. The Indians had learned to earn their livelihood like the whites. In fact, in most ways, the Cherokees now lived just like their American neighbors. The tribe had agreed to lose many of its old ways, but one thing it steadfastly refused to do was lose any more of its territory. Although many Cherokees were willing to live like Americans, they did not want to be Americans. ▲

CHAPTER **5**

The Trail of Tears

The Cherokee constitution caused a serious problem for the American government. In the document, the Cherokees maintained that land in four U.S. states—Georgia, Alabama, Tennessee, and North Carolina—belonged to the tribe. The white settlers in these states were angered by the Indians' claim. They demanded that U.S. officials force the Cherokees to move somewhere else.

The idea of moving the Indians had been discussed in Washington, D.C., for years. In 1803, President Thomas Jefferson first suggested that Indians living in the East should be given land west of the Mississippi

River. He argued that if Indians moved to the West, hundreds of miles away from whites, they would be far happier than if they stayed in the East. In the West, no one would try to "civilize" them. The Indians could live however they chose.

During the "civilization" movement, some Cherokees decided to move to present-day Texas and Arkansas for just this reason. But most Cherokees opposed relocation, which was called *removal*. Why should we have to leave the homeland of our ancestors just to please these white newcomers? they asked. Many Cherokees had already adopted white ways in order to please the government. But they would not give up their land just because white settlers wanted it.

An organized opposition to removal sprang up among the Cherokees. In 1819, the Cherokee council announced that the tribe would sell no more land to the U.S. government. Any Cherokee who signed a treaty granting tribal land to the United States would be sentenced to death.

The Cherokees were determined to stay, but the settlers were just as determined to force them to leave. Whites in Georgia, the state with the largest Cherokee population, were especially eager to see the tribe's removal. When the Cherokees' constitution claimed the tribe owned land in Georgia, the settlers saw a golden opportunity.

The Georgians said that the Cherokees had broken U.S. law by trying to create a state within a state. Using this charge as an excuse, whites began to seize Indian land. Georgia also passed laws abolishing the Cherokee government and court system. The Georgia Guard, a special police force, was formed to punish Cherokees who resisted.

The Indians appealed to the U.S. government for help, but received little response. In fact, President Andrew Jackson supported the Georgians. He told the Cherokees that if they did not like the way they were being treated, they should move west.

Scared about their future, the Cherokees began to fight among themselves. One small group formed the Treaty party. Its members wanted to keep peace with whites above all. They were willing to negotiate a treaty calling for their removal, if necessary. Most Cherokees, however, stood by Chief John Ross, a strong opponent of removal.

The United States ignored the wishes of Ross's many supporters. The government sent representatives to meet with about 100 Treaty party members in December of 1835. The two groups negotiated the Treaty of New Echota. In the treaty, the Cherokees of the Treaty party agreed to give the United States all Cherokee land in the Southeast. In exchange, the Cherokees were to receive a tract of land in present-day northeastern Oklahoma.

The rest of the Cherokees were furious when they learned what the Treaty party had done. Almost 15,000 Cherokees signed a petition saying that they did not agree with the terms of the Treaty of New Echota. But the United States paid them no attention. U.S. officials told the Cherokees that, like it or not, the tribe would have to move west within two years. Now it was the Cherokees' turn to ignore the United States. The tribe refused to prepare to make the move.

In the summer of 1838, the U.S. government decided to remove the Cherokees by

The Trail of Tears, *painted by Robert Lindneux in 1942*

force. U.S. soldiers invaded the Cherokee Nation. They imprisoned many Indians and burned their villages and fields.

One group of Cherokees, who lived along North Carolina's Oconaluftee River, aided the white intruders. The Oconaluftee Cherokees felt that the 1835 removal treaty did not apply to them. They considered themselves citizens of North Carolina rather than members of the Cherokee Nation. With the help of a white man who had been adopted by the Oconaluftees, the group obtained special permission to remain in North Carolina. In return, the Oconaluftees helped the U.S. troops capture a Cherokee named Tsali. Tsali had killed two soldiers who had tried to imprison him when he refused to move to the West.

In order to escape brutal treatment at the hands of the troops, most of the Cherokees finally told the government that they would leave the Southeast. The following winter, the majority of the Cherokee population traveled hundreds of miles to their new home in the West. Their journey is now known as the *Trail of Tears* because of the great suffering they experienced along the way. Given little food or protection against the cold, many Cherokees became sick.

continued on page 57

BEAUTIFUL OBJECTS

Before the invention of machines, all peoples had to make the objects they needed by hand. Some of the items the Cherokees produced helped them perform their daily chores. Among these were the baskets in which they stored food and the pottery in which they cooked their meals. Other items made by the tribe were used only during ceremonies. For example, the Cherokees carved fanciful wooden masks to wear in the booger ritual, a ceremony performed to ridicule the tribe's enemies.

Today, like other Americans, the Cherokees buy most of the goods they use day to day. However, many craftspeople keep the old traditions alive, using the same materials and techniques as did their ancestors to make beautiful objects.

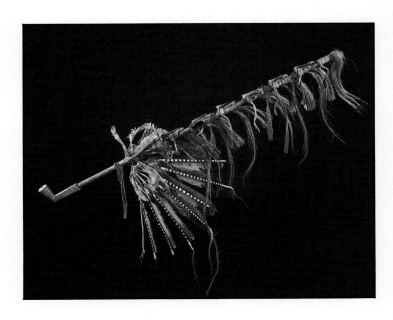

A 19th-century wooden calumet, or peace pipe—attached to a stone bowl—is adorned with feathers, cloth, horsehair, and shells.

A 20th-century Cherokee craftsman carves a booger mask.

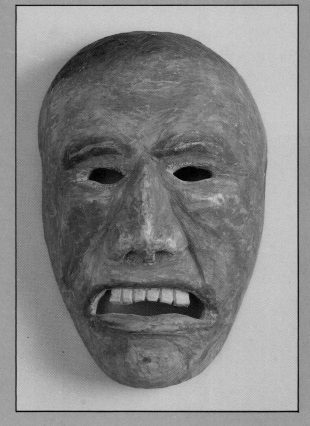

A Cherokee bear's-head mask (above), trimmed with animal fur.

The bared teeth on this wooden booger-mask mock the aggressive grimace of enemy warriors.

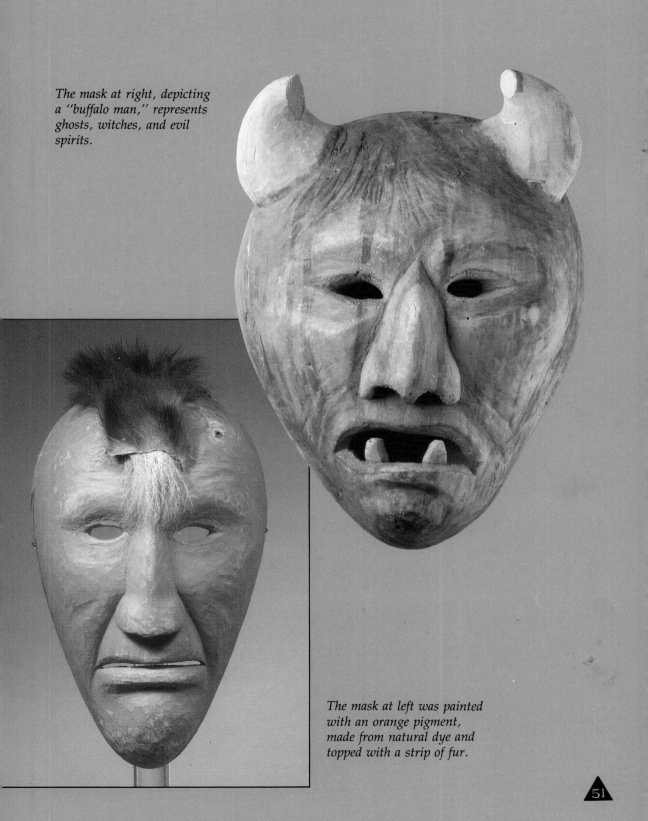

The mask at right, depicting a "buffalo man," represents ghosts, witches, and evil spirits.

The mask at left was painted with an orange pigment, made from natural dye and topped with a strip of fur.

51

A member of the Eastern Band of Cherokee weaves split cane into a basket.

A 19th-century Cherokee basket (below). The handle is a 20th-century addition.

The 19th-century basket
(above) held dried corn or
beans.

A split-cane jar colored with
dye from bloodroots and
walnuts.

A Cherokee potter readies a clay piece for the kiln, where it will be fired, or baked.

This pot with a "weeping eye" motif (above) dates from the Mississippian period (A.D. 700–1540).

The Mississippian piece (left) bears black markings, created when the pottery was fired over a flame.

A Mississippian pot is decorated with a sculpted frog.

This cooking vessel dates after the Mississippian era. It is stamped with a pattern carved from wood.

These pipes, created for daily rather than ceremonial use, feature human figures carved from soapstone, a soft stone with a gray-green hue.

continued from page 48

Possibly as many as half of the Indians on the Trail of Tears did not survive the ordeal. One of the thousands who died was the wife of John Ross. One night she gave her only blanket to a sick child. Wearing little clothing, she continued on, marching through a blinding snowstorm. She caught pneumonia and perished soon afterward.

For many years, the Cherokees had worked hard to adapt to white culture and form a strong Indian nation. The U.S. government had rewarded their efforts with the horrible Trail of Tears. The Western Cherokees who survived now had nothing but a patch of territory in an unfamiliar place and the fading memory of their beautiful homeland. ▲

Stand Watie, a leader of the Treaty party

CHAPTER **6**

Life in the West

In the spring of 1839, the Cherokees who survived the Trail of Tears arrived in the West. They found that they were not alone in their new homeland. Accused of being traitors by their fellow tribespeople, the members of the Treaty party had fled there several years before. Many of the Arkansas Cherokees had also moved westward. These people became known as the Old Settlers.

The Old Settlers and the Treaty party shared the same territory, but they did not like or trust each other. The arrival of the removed Cherokees—called the National party—only made matters worse. Outnumbered by the National party members, both the Old Settlers and the Treaty party feared and resented the newcomers.

Members of the National party and the Old Settlers met to try to resolve their differences in early June of 1839. Unfortunately, nothing was decided other than to have another meeting at a later date. But before this second meeting could take place, the Cherokees' hostilities turned into violence.

On June 22, a group of men dragged John Ridge, the leader of the Treaty party, out of his bed and stabbed him to death while his family looked on. The assassins then murdered two other prominent Treaty party members.

Another member, Stand Watie, managed to escape. He quickly gathered up supporters to help him avenge the murders. It looked as though a full-scale war would break out among the Western Cherokees.

Hoping to prevent more violence, the National party members voted to pardon Ridge's murderers. The members also met with the Old Settlers and drafted a constitution. The constitution stated that the Western Cherokees were one people.

Despite these efforts to arrive at a peaceful solution to their disagreements, fighting began. For seven years, the three Cherokee groups battled each other. Finally, in 1846, John Ross, Stand Watie, and other Cherokee leaders agreed to end the war. The Western Cherokees at last began to work together to create a new Cherokee Nation.

In 1844, the *Cherokee Advocate* was first published. Like the *Phoenix*, the newspaper printed news, editorials, and advertisements in both Cherokee and English. Its motto, Our Rights—Our Country—Our Race, was an inspiration to the emerging Cherokee Nation.

Another of the Western Cherokees' greatest achievements during this time was their public school system. Two schools— one for men, one for women—were established. The school for women was particularly revolutionary. At the time, most Americans believed that women were much less intelligent than men. The Cherokees challenged this view by creating a school that offered women an excellent education.

Most of the Indians made their living in the same ways that whites in the region did. Many Cherokees became successful cattle ranchers and salt merchants. Others were

Students on the lawn of the Cherokee Female Seminary

farmers and plantation owners. By 1860, the Cherokees had 4,000 black slaves. Some of the Indians opposed slavery, however.

The issue of slavery was being debated not just in the Cherokee Nation but throughout the United States. Many Americans in northern states opposed slavery. Some influential people in the South, however, depended on slaves to work their large farms. Angered by the northerners' attempts to outlaw slavery, a group of southern states declared their independence and started a new country, the Confederate States of America. The northern states, known as the Union, decided to fight to keep the South from leaving the United States. In 1861, the first shots rang out, and the Civil War began.

The war caused great conflict among the Western Cherokees. Should they support the Confederacy, helping the same southern states that had forced them off their homeland? Or should they support the Union, which, if it won the war, would make the Cherokees give up their slaves? After much debate, Stand Watie and John Ross decided that the Cherokees should side with the Confederacy.

The Cherokees had taken a stand, but the disagreements among them continued. Cherokees who supported the Union wore two crossed pins under the lapels of their coats as a symbol of their feelings. The Pins, as they became known, started to attack Confederate sympathizers. Stand Watie and his supporters, in turn, assaulted the Pins. The Cherokees' position became even more confused when John Ross shifted his allegiance to the Union. Most of the Western Cherokees thought of Ross as their principal chief. Even though the Cherokees were official allies of the Confederacy, most of the Indians followed Ross's lead and unofficially became Union supporters.

On April 9, 1865, the Civil War ended with a Union victory. The North and the South were to remain united. The Cherokee people, however, were divided. Still, they managed to set aside their differences long enough to sign a peace treaty with the U.S. government. In the treaty, the Western Cherokees agreed to free their slaves, let the Delaware and Shawnee Indians settle on Cherokee territory, and allow railroad companies to build train lines through the center of the Cherokee Nation.

With the railroads came homesteaders—eastern whites looking to build homes and farms on western land. These whites saw that the Cherokees' land along the rail lines was very valuable. Many wanted control of it for themselves.

These people pressured the U.S. government to divide the Indians' territory into

The arrival of the first train in the town of Tahlequah in Western Cherokee territory

small plots, called *allotments*. The Cherokees had always shared all of their land. If the nation were divided into allotments, however, these plots would become the personal property of individual Indians. Whites liked this plan because, after each Cherokee was given an allotment, any extra land would become the property of the United States. The whites knew that the United States would let them buy up this surplus land.

In 1893, the U.S. government sent representatives to the Cherokee Nation. These people were to make a roll, or list, of all of the Cherokees who should receive allotments. The Cherokees were angry. They did not want to allot their land. They wanted to share their territory as they always had.

The United States paid little attention to the Cherokees' resistance. When Cherokee individuals refused to choose an allotment, the U.S. representatives merely assigned them one. In a few years, all the allotments were doled out, and the United States outlawed the Cherokee political system. In 1907, the Western Cherokees became citizens of the new state of Oklahoma. Without their own land or government, the tribe faced the new century with uncertainty. ▲

Wilma Mankiller,
principal chief of the
Cherokee Nation in
Oklahoma

CHAPTER **7**

The Cherokees Today

In the early 1900s, calling oneself a Cherokee could mean many things. Some Cherokees fully embraced the old ways of the tribe. Other Cherokees were Indians by birth but lived much like non-Indians. Still others fell somewhere between these two groups.

Different Cherokees also now had different homelands. For more than 60 years, the Western Cherokees and the Eastern Cherokees had considered themselves separate peoples. The bonds of kinship had so weakened that the Eastern Cherokees had even launched a lawsuit against their western relatives in 1886. The Western Cherokees had kept all the proceeds of the land they were forced to sell to the United States after the Civil War. The Eastern Cherokees claimed that they deserved a share of this money. The court disagreed and awarded them nothing.

The Eastern Cherokees, however, had been able to hold on to much of their land. The Western Cherokees were not so lucky. Many people who received allotments were unfamiliar with the business dealings of non-Indians. A large number of these Cherokee landowners were cheated out of their property by dishonest whites.

The Cherokees in Oklahoma also suffered from not having their own leaders. They still had chiefs, but no longer had the right to choose them. The president instead appointed the Western Cherokees' official "representatives." These appointees rarely had any interest in Cherokee traditions.

One group was so dissatisfied with these leaders that it organized its own council. Led by Red Bird Smith, these Cherokees turned to an ancient religious society, the Keetoowah, for guidance. They refused to accept allotments and retreated into the hills of Oklahoma, where they maintained the traditional Cherokee way of life.

The Eastern Cherokees had likewise long resisted "civilization." They fought to

A typical house of the Eastern Cherokees in North Carolina in the early 1900s

stay in the East because they wanted to live as the Cherokees had long ago, hunting and farming on the land Kana'ti and Selu had once called home. But over time, they had also learned how to deal with the non-Cherokee world. This knowledge helped them establish a profitable business selling timber from the forests of their homeland. They

made a fair amount of money from the timber industry until the mid-1920s. By that time, some whites had illegally got their names on the official roll of Eastern Cherokees. These "white Cherokees" took control of the timber profits. They forced many of the Eastern Cherokees into unemployment and poverty.

During the Great Depression of the 1930s, President Franklin Delano Roosevelt introduced a set of government programs called the New Deal. The New Deal was designed to help all Americans by providing jobs to the many citizens who were out of work. The Eastern Cherokees also profited from the new programs. For 2 weeks each month, approximately 100 Cherokee men worked for the Indian Emergency Conservation Work Program. This project was dedicated to conserving natural resources in North Carolina.

In 1934, the Great Smoky Mountains National Park opened in North Carolina. Located on Cherokee territory, the park allowed the Eastern Cherokees to have daily contact with white Americans from across the country. This interaction and the sale of souvenirs led to new economic and social growth for the Indians' communities.

In 1933, President Roosevelt appointed John Collier as commissioner of Indian affairs. Collier helped to bring about the passage of the Indian Reorganization Act (IRA). Under this act, allotment was ended, the sale of Indian lands was regulated, and $2 million a year was set aside to purchase land for Indians.

Unfortunately, the new act did little for the Cherokees in the East or the West. The Eastern Cherokees continued to be dominated by the "white Cherokees." These people were in favor of individual, rather than tribal, ownership of land. In the West, non-Indian politicians blocked efforts to aid the Cherokees.

Neither the Eastern Cherokees nor the Western Cherokees benefited greatly from the New Deal. But the United States's involvement in World War II (1941–45) did bring important changes to the Indians' lives. More than 1,000 Cherokee men fought alongside other U.S. troops from varied racial and ethnic backgrounds. This experience exposed these Cherokees to new knowledge of American and European society. After the war, many also took advantage of the G.I. Bill of Rights, which allowed veterans to attend college for free.

The Cherokee Gardens in Tahlequah is one of many businesses established recently by Cherokees in Oklahoma.

In the 1950s, the Cherokees started moving to cities. Many were aided by the U.S. government's relocation program. Much like the earlier "civilization" movement, the relocation program grew out of the government's assumption that Native Americans would be better off if they adapted to non-Indian society. At first, adjustment to city life was difficult for many Cherokees. These urban Indians had a hard time finding good-paying jobs and decent housing.

In the late 1950s and 1960s, special government programs slowly improved the living conditions of all Cherokees. The Western Cherokees were also aided by $15 million that they were awarded in a lawsuit against the government. The court agreed with the Indians that the United States had illegally forced them to sell a tract of land in 1893. The Western Cherokees used the money to help pay for the construction of a cultural center and to buy land.

The Cherokees saw even greater changes in the 1970s. In 1970, the Western Cherokees once again won the right to elect their own chiefs. In 1975, they created a new constitution to regulate these elections. These democratic measures helped give new life to the Cherokee Nation.

Many Cherokees who had left Oklahoma were drawn back. One was Wilma Mankiller, a Cherokee woman raised in San Francisco. After moving to Oklahoma in 1975, she became very involved in community projects. In 1985, Mankiller was elected principal chief. She is but one of the

many Cherokees who grew up far from their homeland but are now determined to preserve their culture.

During the 1960s and 1970s, the 8,000 members of the Eastern Band continued to face financial hardships. Less successful

Like their ancestors, the Cherokees of today play stick ball to keep strong and fit.

than their kin in the West, the Eastern Band had to rely on tourism for income. Many of them would "play" the kind of Indian they believed tourists wanted to see. For example, they adopted tipis and warbonnets— two things Cherokees never traditionally used. Recently, though, they have projected a more accurate image of their history and culture.

The Eastern Band became more financially secure in the 1980s. These Cherokees set up a bingo parlor, which created many jobs for Cherokees in the game parlor and in nearby restaurants and motels. In 1987, the Eastern Cherokees' purchase of a mirror-manufacturing firm created another source of income for the tribe.

The Eastern and Western Cherokees live thousands of miles from each other. Yet, many ties remain, through family, friends, and a shared culture. In the beginning, for both, there were Kana'ti and Selu, from whom the Cherokees learned the importance of balance and harmony. They also developed an ability to adapt and change as was needed. Maintaining their culture while absorbing many features of the modern world, the Principal People have created a perfect harmony between their thousand-year-old past and their diverse present. ⬆

CHRONOLOGY

1540   Spanish explorer Hernando de Soto arrives in Cherokee territory

1759   A group of Cherokee chiefs are imprisoned by English soldiers

1776   Cherokees attack American settlements during the Revolutionary War

ca. 1819   Sequoyah completes Cherokee alphabet

1827   First constitution of the Cherokee Nation written

1835   Treaty party members agree to surrender the Cherokee homeland to the United States in the Treaty of New Echota

1838–39   Cherokees journey to present-day Oklahoma on Trail of Tears

1846   Seven-year civil war among the Western Cherokees ends

1861   Western Cherokees become allies of the Confederacy

1907   The Western Cherokees become citizens of Oklahoma

1941–45   More than 1,000 Cherokees serve in U.S. military during World War II

1961   Western Cherokees awarded $15 million in lawsuit against the U.S. government

1985   Wilma Mankiller elected principal chief of the Cherokee Nation in Oklahoma

GLOSSARY

allotment   a U.S. government policy of the late 1800s that sought to divide tribally owned land into small, individually owned tracts; also, a tract of land given to an Indian because of the allotment policy

Ani-Yun'wiya   the name the Cherokees call themselves; can be translated as "Principal People"

"civilization" movement   a campaign by U.S. officials and non-Indian missionaries in the early 1800s to teach the Cherokees to live like white settlers

clan   a large group of relatives who believe they descended from a common ancestor

Green Corn Ceremony   an annual Cherokee celebration traditionally held when the corn crop ripened

Kana'ti   the first man, according to Cherokee legend

removal   a U.S. government policy of the early 1800s that required Indians living in what is now the eastern United States to move to lands west of the Mississippi River

Selu   the first woman, according to Cherokee legend

Trail of Tears   the long, difficult journey the Cherokees made in the mid-1830s from their southeastern homeland to present-day Oklahoma

INDEX

A

Alabama, 43
Allotments, 64–65, 68, 71
American Revolution, 29
Ani-Yun'wiya, 9. *See also* Cherokees
Arkansas, 44, 59

B

Black drink, 19
Boudinot, Elias, 39
Bubonic plague, 24

C

Cherokee Advocate, 61
Cherokee Nation, 39–41, 63, 73
Cherokee Phoenix, 39, 61
Cherokees
    alliance with English, 25
    assimilation into non-Indian culture, 33–39, 34, 43, 67, 68–69, 71, 75
    child rearing, 14
    clothing, 17, 36
    conflicts within tribe, 45–47, 48, 60–61, 63
    crafts, 17
    creation story, 7–9, 11
    education, 36–37, 61
    family structure, 14
    farming, 39
    fishing, 17
    forestry, 69–70
    gender roles, 15–20, 36, 37
    government, 19, 39–41, 45, 68, 73
        constitution, 41, 60
        dissolved by United States, 44, 65
    homeland, 9, 11, 23, 44
    housing, 13–14
    hunting, 17
    land, 39, 61–62, 71

    lawsuits over, 67–68, 73
    loss of, 29–31, 41, 64–65, 68
    language, 37–39
    relocation to cities, 72–73
    spiritual beliefs, 19, 20, 21
    warfare, 19–20, 25, 29
Choctaw Indians, 25
Christianity, 23–24, 36–37
"Civilization" movement, 33–39, 43
Civil War, 62–63, 68
Collier, John, 71
Confederate States of America, 62, 63
Constitution, U.S., 41

D

Darkening Land, 19, 20
Delaware Indians, 64

E

Eastern Cherokees, 67, 70, 71, 75
English, 24, 25, 26, 27, 29
Europe, 71

F

Fort Prince George, 27
France, 25
French and Indian War, 25–29

G

General Council, 41, 44
Georgia, 29, 43, 44–45
Georgia Guard, 45
G.I. Bill of Rights, 71
Great Depression, 70
Great Smoky Mountains National Park, 70
Green Corn Ceremony, 15, 20–21

I

Indian Emergency Conservation Work Program, 70

INDEX

Indian Reorganization Act, 71
Iroquois Indians, 25

J
Jackson, Andrew, 45
Jefferson, Thomas, 43

K
Kana'ti, 8, 11, 69, 75
Keetoowah, 68

L
Lighthorse Guard, 41

M
Mankiller, Wilma, 73–75
Measles, 24
Meigs, Return J., 34, 36
Missionaries and mission
   schools, 36
Mississippi River, 43–44

N
National party, 59, 60
New Deal, 70–71
North Carolina, 29, 43, 48, 70

O
Oconaluftee Cherokees, 48
Oconaluftee River, 48
Oconostota, 27
Ohio River valley, 26
Oklahoma, 11, 68, 73
Old Settlers, 59, 60

P
Pins, 63

R
Railroads, 64
Removal, 45, 48
      resistance to, 44. See also
      Trail of Tears

Ridge, John, 60
Roosevelt, Franklin Delano, 70, 71
Ross, John, 45, 47, 57, 61, 63
Rutherford, Griffith, 29

S
San Francisco, California, 73
Selu, 8, 9, 11, 69, 75
Sequoyah, 37–39
Shawnee Indians, 64
Smallpox, 24
Smith, Red Bird, 68
Soto, Hernando de, 23
South Carolina, 29
Stick ball, 17–18

T
Tennessee, 43
Texas, 44
Trail of Tears, 43–57, 59
Treaty of New Echota, 47
Treaty party, 45, 47, 59, 60
Tsali, 48

U
United States, 9, 11, 29, 31, 33–34,
   36, 41, 43, 44, 45, 47, 57, 62,
   64–65, 71, 72
United States Army, 48, 71

V
Virginia, 29

W
War Women, 20
Washington, D.C., 43
Watie, Stand, 60, 61, 63
Western Cherokees, 59–62,
   63–65, 67, 75
"White Cherokees," 70, 71
Wild Boy, 8, 9
World War II, 71

ABOUT THE AUTHOR

NICOLE CLARO holds a B.A. in literature from Bennington College. She lives in New York City, where she works for the Metropolitan Museum and studies modern dance.

PICTURE CREDITS